Tyrannosaurus Rex

Versus

the Corduroy Kid

Tyrannosaurus Rex

Versus

the Corduroy Kid

SIMON ARMITAGE

ALFRED A. KNOPF   NEW YORK   2008

Library of Congress Cataloguing-in-Publication Data

Armitage, Simon, 1963–
Tyrannosaurus Rex versus the Corduroy Kid / by Simon Armitage.—
1st U.S. ed.
p.   cm.
ISBN 978-0-307-26841-9
I. Title.
PR6051.R564T97 2008
821'.914—dc22
2008014191

Goliath of Gath, with hith helmet of bwath,
wath theated one morning upon the gween gwath,
when up thlipped thlim David, the thervant of Thaul,
who thaid I thall thmite thee, although I'm tho thmall.

—Anon.

Acknowledgments

Acknowledgments are due to the following publications in which some of these poems first appeared: *PN Review*; *Poetry London*; *The Stinging Fly* (Ireland); *Fulcrum* (US); *Times Literary Supplement*; *The Independent*; *The New Republic* (US); *The Rialto*; *The Times*; *The Guardian*; *The Liberal*; *The North*; *Nature*; *Poesia* (Italy); *Marsden Parish Church Magazine*; *Poetry Review*; *Wild Reckoning* (Calouste Gulbenkian Foundation, edited by John Burnside and Maurice Riordan); *Machinery of Grace* (Beverley Minster, Beverley Literature Festival and The Poetry Society); *From Here to Here* (Cyan Books); *Raising the Iron* (Palace Theatre, Watford, edited by David Harsent).

Special thanks are also due to the following individuals and organisations: Janet Whittaker; Drenka Willen; Kate Rowland; Peter Bennet; Paul Keegan; Tom McRae; Mark Radcliffe; Tim Dee; Craig Smith; The British Library; Opera North; 26; BBC Radio 2; BBC Radio 3; BBC Radio 4; BBC 1; W. W. Norton & Company, US; Harcourt, US.

Contents

Tyrannosaurus Rex

Versus

the Corduroy Kid

Hand-Washing Technique—Government Guidelines

i.m. Dr David Kelly

1 Palm to palm.
2 Right palm over left dorsum and left palm over right dorsum.
3 Palm to palm fingers interlaced.
4 Backs of fingers to opposing palms with fingers interlocked.
5 Rotational rubbing of right thumb clasped in left palm and vice versa.
6 Rotational rubbing, backwards and forwards with clasped fingers of right hand in left palm and vice versa.

from The Odyssey

Then all the men came and added their weight,
hammered that burning stake into his head,
and when the eyeball burst we were soaked in ink,
and the lens crunched and cracked like splintering ice,
and the lashes and eyebrows flared like burning grass,
and we leaned, and heaved, and forced it further in
until the retina sheared, and the optic nerve
spat and seared and spasmed and fused in the heat.
All the while he screamed into the cave,
roared his pain into the booming, echoing rock,
so loud that other one-eyed monsters on the island
came to listen. They gathered outside, more curious
than concerned, and shouted, "Hey, you in there,
what's all the fuss and palaver? Who's giving you grief?"
And Cyclops, writhing in pain, his head in flames, shouted,
"Nobody. Nobody hurts Cyclops. Nobody."
So they shrugged their shoulders and padded off home.
A master-stroke on my part, and it worked.
When we drew out the stake it was like a bung,
like a cork, like a plug—blood spurted and plumed,
but I didn't finish him off, the thick-headed brute. Why?
He'd rolled a stone into the cave's mouth, blocking the gap,
a stone so vast that he alone could shift it from the hole.
And this is the point of my ingenious plan.
The flock were cowering away from the noise and flames.
Twines and twisted willow-strands littered the floor.

Each man lashed himself tight under a fat ram,
and two other rams were tethered alongside
to shield him at the flanks as he dangled and clung on.

Then they ambled forward, tottered over the stone floor,
bleated to be let out of the cave for water and pasture,
and Cyclops, even with a smoking hole instead of an eye
was still a shepherd at heart, so he rolled away the rock,
opened the mouth of the cave and counted them out,
"mether, tether, mimph, hither, lither, anver, danver . . ."
stroking their backs as they wandered into the light.
The ignorant swine, he released them one at a time,
each big ram with one of my men slung under its gut.
And I was the last man to escape, suspended beneath
the cockiest ram of the lot, my fingers twisted
into the deep shag of his coat, my feet stirruped
in the swags of elastic skin to the inside of his leg.

Once on the boats with the men and the flock
and the buckets of cheeses and barrels of milk
I goaded old one-eye with taunts, and he hurled rocks
from the cliff but they only caused ripples
that pushed us further to sea. The wide open sea.

And the men cheered and laughed until light . . .
when it dawned on us that nothing had changed.

Still lost, still famished-hearted, still years from home,
but now with Poseidon fuming and writhing below,
plotting revenge for blinding his one-eyed son.

That act was to haunt us. From then on
we were marked men, locked on a collision course
with the God of the Sea. He lurked in the depths,
a constant presence. We sensed him under the waves.
The boat shivered when he stirred. And if we'd have known
the chain of events we'd set in place, the cruelty

and agony that stretched ahead, year after year,
the horror and terror and sadness and loss still to come—
    who knows,
perhaps we'd have chosen to die right there, in the black
    cave,
out of sight of heaven and without sound.

We drifted on wind and current, hoping again,
hoping against hope, praying, looking for land.

KX

Northerner, this is your stop. This longhouse
of echoing echoes and sooted glass,
this goth pigeon hangar, this diesel roost
is the end of the line. Brace and be brisk,
commoner, carry your heart like an egg
on a spoon, be fleet through the concourse, primed
for that point in time when the world goes bust,
when the unattended holdall or case
unloads its cache of fanaticised heat.

Here's you after the fact, found by torchlight,
being-less, heaped, boned of all thought and sense.
The camera can barely look. Or maybe,
just maybe, you live. Here's you on the News,
shirtless, minus a limb, exiting smoke
to a backdrop of red melt, onto streets
paved with gilt, begging a junkie for help.

On Marsden Moor

Above the tree line and below the fog
I watched two men on the opposite slope
hauling wooden poles and slabs of dressed stone
from the foot of the hill towards the top.

They didn't stall—just lifted, carried, dropped.
I watched for an hour or thereabouts,
way off, but close enough in a straight line
to bundle them over with a big shout.

Away from the five o'clock of the town,
out from under the axles and bruised skies
it bothered me that men should hike this far
to hoik timber and rock up a steep bank.

Because what if those poles were fencing posts
to hammer home, divide a plot of land
between the two of them, and those dumb stones
the first steps to a new Jerusalem?

Horses, M62

Sprung from a field,
a team
of a dozen or so

is suddenly here and amongst,
silhouettes
in the butterscotch dusk.

One ghosts
between vans,
traverses three lanes,

its chess-piece head
fording the river of fumes;
one jumps the barricades

between carriageways;
a third slows
to a halt

then bends, nosing
the road, tonguing the surface
for salt.

Standstill.
Motor oil pulses.
Black blood.

Some trucker
swings down from his cab
to muster and drove; but

unbiddable, crossbred nags
they scatter
through ginnels

of coachwork and chrome,
and are distant, gone,
then a dunch

and here alongside
is a horse,
the writhing mat of its hide

pressed on the glass—
a tank of worms—
a flank

of actual horse . . .
It bolts,
all arse and tail

through a valley
of fleet saloons.
Regrouped they clatter away,

then spooked by a horn
double back,
a riderless charge,

a flack of horseshoe and hoof
into the idling cars,
now eyeball, nostril, tooth

under the sodium glow,
biblical, eastbound,
against the flow.

Defrosting a Chicken

He was spark out, but at noon, on the beach,
entertained the thought that a fly might land
on a tingle of nerves, just beyond reach.
Save him connecting his brain to his hand.

Donkeys down on the shore were refugees
or latter-day saints, and along Pine Walk
pines grew obliquely, charmed by the salt breeze.
Wax-coated needles wouldn't sink. Loose talk.

On the prom, retired expatriates swarmed
around shrinkwrapped heaps of the *Daily Mail*.
Waves were never the tide but ripples, spawned
by moon-coloured ships of war. The sun's nail

by dusk—rusty, blunt—useless against ice.
For supper he ate the sleep from his eyes.

A Vision

The future was a beautiful place, once.
Remember the full-blown balsa-wood town
on public display in the Civic Hall?
The ring-bound sketches, artists' impressions,

blueprints of smoked glass and tubular steel,
board-game suburbs, modes of transportation
like fairground rides or executive toys.
Cities like *dreams,* cantilevered by light.

And people like us at the bottle bank
next to the cycle path, or dog-walking
over tended strips of fuzzy-felt grass,
or model drivers, motoring home in

electric cars. Or after the late show—
strolling the boulevard. They were the plans,
all underwritten in the neat left-hand
of architects—a true, legible script.

I pulled that future out of the north wind
at the landfill site, stamped with today's date,
riding the air with other such futures,
all unlived in and now fully extinct.

Causeway

Three walked barefoot into the sea,
mother, father and only child
with trousers rolled above the knee.
A stretch of water—half a mile;
granite loaves made a cobbled road
when the tide was low. Tide was high.
Bread vans idled on either shore.
In lifeboat sheds along the coast
cradled boats were dead to the world—
the bones of reassembled whales.
A mothballed helicopter dozed.
But three unshod went wading on,
father, mother and little one,
up to their hips in brine and krill,
the Gulf Stream nudging at their heels,
husband, wife and three-year-old,
out of their depth and further still,
over their heads in surf and swell,
further, further, under then gone.
The life guard yawned a megaphone.
The oyster-catcher clenched its fist.
The common dolphin bit its lip.
The paraglider pulled away.
The scuba diver held his breath.
Then three appeared. Two heads at first
and then the third, now figurines
emergent, shoeless, plodding on
towards the slipway and the quay.
Three forms. They stopped and turned and faced.
So hundreds followed in their wake,
some on Zimmer frames, some on stilts,
some in wellies and some on bikes,
one with gravy stains up his tie;
thousands legging it down the beach,

some in khaki and some in kilts,
some in purdah and fancy dress,
one with a monkey round his neck.
And more. In fact the bastard lot.
(Two rivers, west and east, now burst
with caribou and wildebeest.)
And woman, man and only child,
the three with trousers rolled who strolled
across the bay, were cast in bronze—
barefoot, blameless, set to stand
above the millions who drowned.

The Six Comeuppances

My mind was like a tree full of monkeys.
Every night, I left a peeled banana
by the bedside table, but by morning
apes galore guffawed from the top branches.

I was all over the place, like the shit
of a mad person. I needed to be
more like a mountain, at one with itself,
and less like a man in a red sports car.

Heaven—the roar of a throaty exhaust
in a long tunnel! But that was the past.
After thousands of miles and umpteen tanks
of petrol, smooth roads turned into cart tracks.

Parked by a milky river, I switched off
and dropped the keys in the frostbitten mitts
of a snow-blind Sherpa. With his one, good
finger, he pointed to smoke in the hills,

where I could live in true freedom with guys
in rabbit-fur coats and goatskin slippers,
penning neat one-liners and platitudes
for Christmas crackers and fortune cookies.

At these dizzy heights, mild hypoxia
fuddles the brain, hence the afternoon naps
and Tarzan dreams. I pick and eat my fleas,
sleep in a bald tyre swung from an old beam.

For every learning curve, a plateau phase.
For every dish of the day, a sell-by date.
A backlash to every latest craze.

A riptide to every seventh wave.
For every moment of truth, an afterthought.
For every miracle cure, an antidote.

You're Beautiful

because you're classically trained.
I'm ugly because I associate piano wire with strangulation.

You're beautiful because you stop to read the cards in
    newsagents' windows about lost cats and missing dogs.
I'm ugly because of what I did to that jellyfish with a lolly
    stick and a big stone.

You're beautiful because for you, politeness is instinctive, not
    a marketing campaign.
I'm ugly because desperation is impossible to hide.

> *Ugly like he is,*
> *Beautiful like hers,*
> *Beautiful like Venus,*
> *Ugly like his,*
> *Beautiful like she is,*
> *Ugly like Mars.*

You're beautiful because you believe in coincidence and the
    power of thought.
I'm ugly because I proved God to be a mathematical
    impossibility.

You're beautiful because you prefer home-made soup to the
    packet stuff.
I'm ugly because once, at a dinner party, I defended the
    aristocracy and wasn't even drunk.

You're beautiful because you can't work the remote control.
I'm ugly because of satellite television and twenty-four-hour
    rolling news.

Ugly like he is,
Beautiful like hers,
Beautiful like Venus,
Ugly like his,
Beautiful like she is,
Ugly like Mars.

You're beautiful because you cry at weddings as well as
funerals.
I'm ugly because I think of children as another species from
a different world.

You're beautiful because you look great in any colour
including red.
I'm ugly because I think shopping is strictly for the
acquisition of material goods.

You're beautiful because when you were born, undiscovered
planets lined up to peep over the rim of your cradle and lay
gifts of gravity and light at your miniature feet.
I'm ugly for saying "love at first sight" is another form of
mistaken identity, and that the most human of all responses
is to gloat.

Ugly like he is,
Beautiful like hers,
Beautiful like Venus,
Ugly like his,
Beautiful like she is,
Ugly like Mars.

You're beautiful because you've never seen the inside of a
car-wash.
I'm ugly because I always ask for a receipt.

You're beautiful for sending a box of shoes to the third
   world.
I'm ugly because I remember the telephone numbers of
   ex-girlfriends and the year Schubert was born.

You're beautiful because you sponsored a parrot in a zoo.
I'm ugly because when I sigh it's like the slow collapse of a
   circus tent.

   Ugly like he is,
   Beautiful like hers,
   Beautiful like Venus,
   Ugly like his,
   Beautiful like she is,
   Ugly like Mars.

You're beautiful because you can point at a man in a uniform
   and laugh.
I'm ugly because I was a police informer in a previous life.

You're beautiful because you drink a litre of water and eat
   three pieces of fruit a day.
I'm ugly for taking the line that a meal without meat is a
   beautiful woman with one eye.

You're beautiful because you don't see love as a competition
   and you know how to lose.
I'm ugly because I kissed the FA Cup then held it up to the
   crowd.

You're beautiful because of a single buttercup in the top
   buttonhole of your cardigan.
I'm ugly because I said the World's Strongest Woman was a
   muscleman in a dress.

You're beautiful because you couldn't live in a lighthouse.
I'm ugly for making hand-shadows in front of the giant bulb,
   so when they look up, the captains of vessels in distress see
   the ears of a rabbit, or the eye of a fox, or the legs of a
   galloping black horse.

> *Ugly like he is,*
> *Beautiful like hers,*
> *Beautiful like Venus,*
> *Ugly like his,*
> *Beautiful like she is,*
> *Ugly like Mars.*

> *Ugly like he is,*
> *Beautiful like hers,*
> *Beautiful like Venus,*
> *Ugly like his,*
> *Beautiful like she is,*
> *Ugly like Mars.*

To the Women of the Merrie England
Coffee Houses, Huddersfield

O women of the Merrie England Coffee Houses, Huddersfield,
when I break sweat just thinking about hard work, I think
about you.
Nowhere to hide behind that counter, nowhere to shirk.
I'm watching you right now bumping and grinding hip to hip,
I'm noting your scrubbed, pink hands in the cabinet of fancy
cakes,
loose and quick among the lemon meringues and cream puffs
and custard tarts, darting and brushing like carp in a glass
tank.

O women, the soles of your feet on fire in your sensible shoes,
your fingers aflame, spitting and hissing under the grill.
You, madam, by the cauldron of soup—you didn't hassle us,
just wiped the crumbs from under our genius poems,
me and the boy Smith, one toasted teacake between us,
eking it out though the dead afternoons, our early drafts
hallmarked and franked with rings of coffee and tea.

Women of the Merrie England, under those scarlet aprons are
you naked?
Are you calendar girls? Miss July traps a swarm of steam in a
jug
as perspiration rolls from the upper delta of her open neck
to where Christ crucified bobs and twists on a gold chain.
Miss April delivers the kiss of life to a Silk Cut by the fire
escape.
Miss November, pass me the key to the toilets, please,
I won't violate your paintwork, desecrate the back of the door

with crude anatomical shapes or the names of speedway stars.
I'm no closet queen in search of a glory hole for gay sex,
no smackhead needing a cubbyhole to shoot up—
one glass of your phosphorescing, radio-active orange crush

was always enough for me and the boy Smith, his mother
asleep at the wheel on the long drive back from Wales,
the airbag not invented yet—just a bubble in somebody's
    dream.

Does he pay you a pittance in groats, King Henry, stuffing his
    face
with hare and swan, his beard dyed red with venison blood
and pinned with the fiddling bones of partridge and quail,
while you, O women of the Merrie England, his maids,
swab the greasy tiles with a bucket of rain and a bald mop
or check for counterfeit tenners under the sun-tanning light?
A tenner!—still two hours' graft at the minimum wage.

Don't let catering margarine ease off your eternity rings.
Don't loose your marriages down the waste-disposal pipe.
Hang on to your husbands and friends—no sugar daddies or
    lovers
or cafetières for you, O women of the Merrie England,
no camomile or Earl Grey, just take-it-or-leave-it ground or
    char
served in the time-bitten cups my grandmother sipped from,
hooking the milky membrane aside with a spoon, watching it
    reform.

I've seen you nudging and winking. Look who just dropped
    in, you say,
The Man Who Fell to Earth, wanting tea for one and the
    soup of the day.
I take the window seat and gawp at the steeplejacks: all gone—
Kendall's, the Coach House, Leeds Road, the White Lion and
    the Yards.
But you, under the mock Tudor beams, under the fake shields,
under the falsified coats of arms, you go on, you go on
O women of the Merrie England, O mothers of Huddersfield,
    O ladies!

The Clown Punk

Driving home through the shonky side of town,
three times out of ten you'll see the town clown,
like a basket of washing that got up
and walked, towing a dog on a rope. But

don't laugh: every pixel of that man's skin
is shot through with indelible ink;
as he steps out at the traffic lights,
think what he'll look like in thirty years' time—

the deflated face and shrunken scalp
still daubed with the sad tattoos of high punk.
You kids in the back seat who wince and scream
when he slathers his daft mush on the windscreen,

remember the clown punk with his dyed brain,
then picture windscreen wipers, and let it rain.

The Slaughtered Lamb

Castrating irons
above the bar—
one pair. A dart,

mid-flight,
suspended
in the deep-fried air.

Two pickled eggs
—your eyes—
in a glass jar.

Your ears—
pork scratchings
on a stone floor.

Eat a lemon,
a full one,
for a free half;

for a pint,
pocket the 8 ball
in the roof of the mouth.

A jukebox
swallows your money
then plays dead.

A local
hammers a coin of the realm
into a turnip.

Into your head.

The Perverts

We cornered one coming out of the gym.
Now everyone feels a whole lot better.
We held a buttercup under his chin,
made him kneel, asked him if he liked butter.

Sympathy

Remember the case of the girl who drowned?
All that she left—an inflatable moon.
The cops in a boat on the lake at night,
trawling for stars. Divers dredging the mud.
And the boy on the bank, his fish-shaped lips
to the silver balloon, breathing her in . . .

*

Anyways, on t'morning after t'party
I trogs downstairs, still bolloxed, and gives t'pantry
t'Hans Blix, lookin' for brain-numbin' drugs. None found.
Full damage report: post-operative breakfast bar;
kitchen a breaker's yard; crustified gunk in all sinks;
bottle of 'aemorrhaged red on its side in a slick;
Aberfan-meets-Mexican-mudslide toilet bowl;
one punctured bean bag spewin' small-bore Styrofoam;
one busted 'eirloom; keyhole blobbed with chuddie gum.
Some skunked-up no-mark buttons 'is coat and 'e's gone.

One ash-trayed reefer two-thirds good. There is a god.
I sparks up. And stands with mi 'ands in mi sleeves, like,
straight-jacket style, and there's this sunken balloon, right,
'alf puffed, skin gone limp and sad. And I'm on mi tod.
So I loosens t'little rubber belly knot
and works open t'valve with mi teeth and mi tongue
and takes a long 'ard pull, draggin' it all back.
But this weren't breath what you'd blown from your own lungs,
this was 'elium-filled, so when I curses your name
it weren't THE ANGRY MAN but Mickey Mouse what spoke.

So I blows it up again, and this time it's smoke.

Sympathy

After the verdict, the murdered man's twin
was suddenly there on the courthouse steps.
He said nothing, just calmly unbuttoned
his jacket and shirt, revealing a vest.
In red, it read Matthew, 5:38.
Then he re-buttoned his suit and he went.

*

*Well, I 'unted 'im down to a council estate
on t'side on an 'ill. Burnt out Vauxall Nova
for a garden shed, one dead cooker on t'lawn,
that kinda thing. It's dark. So I gets t'car jack
out of t'boot and jemmies t'window casin'—
wood were rotten, putty gone to shot—and slides in.
Dog-leg stairs. Dog-piss carpet. Dog-ends all over t'shop.
'E's sat on 'is bed doin' X-Box with 'is thumbs.
Looks up and sees me lollin' in t'door 'ole. Sees t'gun.
I stands there a minute, clockin' 'im. You know t'sort:*

*Mettallica T-shirt, trainers, camouflage shorts,
number-four cropped curly 'air and pony-tail,
tatts on 'is forearms. Cackin' 'imself, I could tell.
"What?" 'e's at it. "What?" Then, "Don't, man. Don't be a cunt."
I lifts t'barrel level with 'is face, and I pulls.
But it weren't lead shot what peppered 'is stupid 'ead—
I'd emptied t'cartridge at 'ome, and loaded up
with ashes instead. Me bruvver's. What they'd givved us
to take 'ome in a brass urn. Then I turns and walks,
leaves 'im with a powdered face and white frightened 'air*

like what those 'igh court judges wear. I got three year.

Sympathy

Remember the case of the birth-marked girl,
a port-wine stain splashed all over her face.
Her parents banned all mirrors from the house,
blinkered her every glance till she was three,
then caught her staring one night, face to face
with the turned-off TV, touching the screen.

*

When she were born she were just as a china doll.
'Ere's a photo we took an 'our after 'er birth—
not a mark on 'er, like a moon afloat in a lake.
Then after a few week she started to blush up.
Like it were growin' underneath, comin' to ripe,
then purple angry, then black like a cloud, then red,
same as one of those commie countries in an old map.
Like she'd tekken a lit firework full in 'er face.
Couldn't bear to touch it it looked so pained.
Dabbed it with cotton wool like it might wipe away.

Then we wondered if it were summat we'd done wrong;
that Sunday tea when 'er mother were six months gone
and I slopped that punnet of strawbs on t'tablecloth.
Or for catchin' on a month before we were wed.
'Ard for a boy, but death on a stick for a girl.
Them nursery kids called 'er squashed tomato 'ed.
Arm, thigh, under 'er foot, anywhere but 'er face.
At night, I used to snug down next to 'er in bed,
put mi face right cheek to cheek, so as while she slept
that bloody patch of rare steak raw flesh might transfer

and blemish me for me sins. Punish me, not 'er.

Sympathy

Remember the man who mounted the kerb
in his car? He was racing a black cloud,
outrunning a dark belt of summer rain
in his soft-top Merc with the roof rolled down.
They found it scrubbed and buffed, spotless except
one pixel of blood on the number plate.

*

Well 'e walked. No jail. 'E strolls out of court scot free,
flashbulbs poppin' like fuck like it were Oscars night,
furry microphones pushed at 'is gob for a quote.
"No comment," 'e mumbles, and jumps in a black cab.
'E'd been in a dodgy bar in town, splashin' out
on oysters and lap-dancin' girls, but 'e weren't pissed.
And 'is licence were clean—it were folded and tucked
in 'is wallet, next to shots of 'is wife and kids,
kept close to 'is 'eart. 'E flashed 'em around in court
like aces. A strong 'and. 'E were a family man.

Instead, 'e's put on some kind of parole. A joke,
'cept there's this one condition: twenny-four-seven
'e carries that wallet. It's brown and it's leather
and opens out, gatefold-like, like a birthday card,
with two little windows inside for family snaps.
So whenever 'e shells out we're right in 'is face:
on one side a photo of me, mi 'air tied up
in a bun, thick mascara, bit of lippy on,
laid in t'coffin, dead as a statue, clock cold;
on t'other mi unborn babe in a tight ball,

sonogram scan, black and white, twenny-eight weeks old.

Sympathy

Remember the case of the birthday bird?
Not a blue macaw on a golden perch
or a budgerigar or zebra finch.
But a pigeon, in fact—a Bleeding Heart Dove.
The one with the seemingly bloodstained chest,
with heartbreak splattered all over its breast.

*

*Meanin' what? That it's all sham? That to watch me mope
you'd think I'd been shot, when really I'm right as rain?
Like I've got this painted-on 'urt, to make folk think
I'm damaged inside, when really I'm really fine?
It sat in mi garden shed not makin' a muff,
till I couldn't cope. I stomped in and bagged it up,
lugged it over to Scapegoat 'ill and shooed it off.
But bugger me sideways! Back at mine it were lodged
on mi windowsill, struttin' its big, bleedin' 'eart stuff.
I coaxed it into mi 'ands with Weetabix crumbs.*

*Took an age to pluck—big pillow-fight-feather-fest
like when that dog-fox ran amuck in Redfearn's coop.
And sure, it weren't blood-marked at all under its coat.
But its crop were burstin' with undigested corn.
I jugged t'lot, steeped it all day on a low light
and washed it down with a bottle of blanc de blanc.
Then ransacked t'carcass for t'wishbone and t'parson's nose.
Then slumped in front of t'telly watchin' UK Gold,
matchstick toothpick in one, remote in t'other 'and,
with mi shirt unbuttoned right down to mi belt, choc flup,*

waitin' for t'exit wound, waitin' for t'blood to pump.

Landfall

This day
weeds floating alongside and also leaves.
A good sign.
Then branches, even a log. Mr. Kid
with his keen nose detects the scent of pine.

This day
bold cloud formations and rain without wind.
A good sign.
Then dry. Then a damp, tubercular breeze.
Then reports that Kid had swallowed a bee.

This day
a tame bird was caught by hand. Feet un-webbed.
A good sign.
Examined, its droppings revealed not fish
but seed. We rolled dice for the roasted breast.

This day
toothache and nosebleeds reported by Kid.
A good sign.
His feet swell in the nearness of sharp rocks
and once, in range of home, he stooled himself.

This day
a brown, four-limbed beast face-down in the waves.
A good sign.
Short-haired. Leather, upturned palms. Five-toed.
It broke apart when spiked with the long hook.

This day
the fifth day of mist, but mingled with smoke.
A good sign.

A coal-cellar sky devoid of moon or stars.
All night Mr. Kid kept watch with his ears.

Then dawn
and black cliffs on the port side. Land ahoy.
A godsend,
but also a cold, late fear, that its dark mass
had skirted us parallel all this week.

This day
a great sight—green mountains loom in the fog.
Poor Kid,
blind from birth, he breaks with tears when he hears.
Stand by with the book of names and the flag.

Surtsey

The smoke hadn't cleared. And the liquid stone
had barely set when a microbe blew in,
press-ganged by wind squeezed out of the west,
a filibustered jot to be dashed and smeared
on this island's reluctant agar plate.
Then nano-dot spiders fell from the sky
and flies crash-landed on its landing pad.
It was nature, alright, its building blocks:
the early empires of lichen and moss,
the stowaway seeds, spores that piggy-backed here
on the bristled skin of a mermaid's purse.
And the crust of the land had hardly cooled
when a plant took root and the beach was stamped
with the three-pronged print of a seagull's boot.

And suddenly man leapt out of his boat,
waded ashore, stumbled along the strand
with fancy gizmos for getting the gist
and GPS in the palm of his hand.
And up went the hut and up went the flag.

Then overnight, on the ness to the north,
a net-float ran aground, metal and round
with blue-green barnacles gummed to its crown,
a faceless, iron ball, big as a head.
By noon it was named, then mounted and raised
on a bleached, driftwood log. Deaf, dumb and blind,
and brainless, but nevertheless, the first god.

Gifted, precocious sprog, right from day one
you were the boy-god: an object lesson
in all that exists, Darwin's dream come true.

You sprouted seaweed and the cameras clicked.
Every birthday you were your own cake.
You were John Craven's favourite wet dream.

Surtsey, Surtsey, have you grown old with grace,
with kittiwake nests and grass in your cliffs?
Or are you the Island of Lost Child Stars:

grandmasters of chess in Clark's shoes and shorts;
Communist gymnasts; squeaking choristers;
bum-fluffed brain-box kids in National Health specs;

the pigtailed, freckled, fallen idols of stage
and screen with puppy-dog eyes and braced teeth.
Surtsey, whose fame could be seen from space,

when I'm winched down under the rotor blade
forty years after the year of our birth,
should I bring beer and cigars, or sherbet

and soft toys? Will it be just razorbills
and me, or will I be met on the quay
by Test Card Girl and the Milky Bar Kid

and a waist-high mob of bickering brats,
to be led by the sleeve along that coast
where all the world's wunderkinder are washed up.

English flags   to be downed.

Harold killed   and (killed) again.

My first man opens his gut with a lance   for lying to France.
My second man lops   the (sceptre and orb)
from between his legs   for lying to fellow men.
My third man cuts out his heart,   for lying to God.
My last man hacks off his (bonce)   for lying to my face.
Leave him, (I say,)   with the ordinary dead.
Food for the (corvine.)   Fishing bait.

The(n) nightfall.   Aftermath.
Victory   is a (new) country.
Once battle subsides, a   (numbness) enters the mind.
England (its crown and throne)   are mine,
but the dead (litter) its soil.   Such (spoil).
(Like a) human forest   ripped into and stormed.

Noblemen lie with commoners,   swineherds (sprawl)
with the (wreckage)   of knights and earls,
the blood of the highborn (clots)   with the blood of the low.

Steam lifts from the bodies,   releasing each (soul)
into the   (next realm.)
These (are the) hours between,   neither loss nor gain.

I (shrug) off my coat of mail,   skin without bone.
Fires are lit with the (kindling) of war   splintered arrows burn.
Men   feast, sup, sing.
I crack the seal from a cask   pour the (melted) Alps,
(clear/pure/sweet)   in my eyes, (on my cheeks/my lips).

Outside,   ghostly women appear,
(as) English   (as) rag dolls,
gleaning   the field.
They   pick through the dead.
One woman broddles   a dead man's head with a stick,
falls,   weeps.

I sleep. (God)   spares me dreams. I sleep.

At dawn a messenger   comes to my tent.
Word (from the) north,   Harold's mother, offering gold
of (his) earthly weight   in return for his corpse.
What bitch is this   who (values) her son
as (cuts of)   meat?

Tell her (")What death has bought   cannot be resold.
What fortune she owns   will be (pocketed) soon.(")

His scattered limbs   could have dropped from the sky.
A woman is called,   (one of his) Saxon whores
—corn hair, bluestone eyes   the neck of a swan.
"This is his head. This his chest,   (these are) his feet.
This is a scar from birth.   This mole on his breast.
These the gouges and bites   (of my) nails and teeth
where I   (loved him) back."

If a body or mind   was a land, it was his.
Parcelled in rough, purple cloth   we cart him
coastwards   (to) under the cliff.
Beach stones are piled   (in a) godless heap.

A grave on a shore   is a (one-night) fuck.
What the crabs leave   the waves sweep clean.
No(thing) remains.   History is mine.
England is France   in (all but) memory and name.

Republic

On Mondays, red cars only enter town.
This is the system. Through the pollution
the snarl-ups, tailbacks and honking of horns
can be mistaken for revolution.

On Tuesdays, white cars alone hit the road.
Looked at from spy satellites it has snowed.
Tourists take photos of convoys winding
along avenues, thinking them weddings.

Blue Wednesday. Blue like the president's blood.
From the mountains the streets are streams in flood.
Thirty degrees in the shade. Armed police
clamp down on turquoise and aquamarine.

Thursday and Fridays are lemon and lime
like the shorts and shirts of the national team
and the national sport is the people's game.
Weekends are free. Purple. Coffee and cream.

And the money rolls by in dark limos.
Raybans flash from behind tinted windows.
Bodywork gleams. The metallic black
shines to a depth where all colours shine back.

Twist

The spotlight threw its custard pie and missed.
A wench in a bodice sold fancy sweets;

slung from her neck, the tray of Walnut Whips
stood in the shadow of her powdered breasts.

The Widow Corney, sherry on her breath,
popped Tic-Tacs in the wings. The chorus line

smoked musky roll-ups on the fire escape.
A mutt with stage fright, Bullseye flinched and pissed

when Bill Sykes raised his stick to Nancy's face.
Three make-up ladies dusted Fagin's schnoz,

un-reconstructed and pre-holocaust.
His cutpurse gang were roughnecks in real life:

between dress rehearsal and opening night
the Artful Dodger had pointed his knife

at Oliver's voice—unbroken and choice—
asked if his balls had dropped, fucked with his head

till the Adam's apple in pretty boy's throat—
quavering, ripe—hung by a slender thread.

Evening

You're twelve. Thirteen at most.
You're leaving the house by the back door.
There's still time. You've promised
not to be long, not to go far.

One day you'll learn the names of the trees.
You fork left under the ridge,
pick up the bridleway between two streams.
Here is Wool Clough. Here is Royd Edge.

The peak still lit by sun. But
evening. Evening overtakes you up the slope.
Dusk walks its fingers up the knuckles of your spine.
Turn on your heel. Back home

your child sleeps in her bed, too big for a cot.
Your wife makes and mends under the light.
You're sorry. You thought
it was early. How did it get so late?

Roadshow

We were drawn uphill by the noise and light:
a silver, extraterrestrial glow
beyond the hill's head; a deep, cardio-
vascular bass in the hill's hollow chest.

We were heavy and slow, each footstep checked
by the pendulum of our unborn child—
a counterweight swinging from Susan's heart.

Day-glo arrows nailed to fences and trees
pointed the way, first along sea-view streets,
past windows dressed with mail-order driftwood
and No Vacancies signs, then a sharp right
through a housing estate where locals emerged
from hedges and gates, pushing tabs and wraps.
Nothing for us.
                    So the road levels out.
But the moment we set foot in the park
the lights are cut and the music fades. And

by pure chance, it's precisely at this point
that the universe—having expanded since birth—
reaches its limit and starts to contract.

The crowd dopples past. The crowd pushes on
to nightclubs and fire-holes down in the bay,
inexhaustibly young and countless strong,
streaming away, always streaming away.

Sloth

As chance would have it, one has come to rest
in the attic room, right over my desk.
Upside down, he hangs from the curtain pole
like a shot beast carried home from the hunt,

but light burns in his eyes; he isn't dead.
A contemplative soul, much like I am,
he's thinking things through, atom by atom,
and hasn't touched the dried fruit and mixed nuts

I left on a plate on the windowsill,
although a mountain range of Toblerone
is thus far unaccounted for. My wife,
the three-times Olympian pentathlete,

wants to trigger his brains with smelling salts,
clip jump-leads on to the lobes of his ears,
stick a bomb up his arse. But I'm not sure:
to me the creature looks dazzled or dazed,

like the Big Bang threw him out of his bed,
like evolution took him by surprise.
Those eyes . . . He can stay another week,
till the weather turns. But now back to work:

look, a giant tortoise goes past in a blur.

Poem on His Birthday

I

Is he an undiscovered species living deep in the rain forests of Borneo, or is he extinct?

II

They pass him through the boughs of a maple tree to ensure a long life. Thanks for that.

III

The planets queue up to take the piss—especially the big ones made of inhospitable gas.

IV

Dogs come up to him and sniff. Their owners call them away.

V

He is banned from the front seat of the car for taking huge bites out of the steering wheel.

VI

He lifted the seashell to his ear as they said he should, and heard whispers and black lies.

VII

Two dozen waxwings on the rotary drier. Meaning what?

VIII

Who carried his crib into the house before he was born?

IX

Those kids collecting dead wood for the bonfire keep looking his way.

X

They pull a small boy out of the earthquake after three weeks, but what use is that to him?

XI

A black beetle scuttles over the living room floor, but it's hard to murder your own.

XII

As an adolescent he enjoyed the company of orchards and streams.

XIII

What's worse? A malignant melanoma or thick black hairs growing out of a facial mole?

XIV

Lord, the butterfly that is his soul only flies while he sleeps.

XV

The ravens have left the tower. Rooks have deserted the dead elm.

XVI

He brings out the worst in people. Why aren't the Army beating a path to his door?

XVII

A soluble aspirin uncoiling in a single malt.

XVIII

He wears a Brazilian football shirt to cover the lack of muscle definition on his upper arms.

XIX

Count your friends using Roman numerals—it makes the total number seem more.

XX

He bought an eternity ring forged from a coffin hinge.

XXI

The sun obscured by cloud—his line manager laughing behind her hand.

XXII

He loves his country but she committed adultery with a man called London.

XXIII

The Personnel Department—their collective smirk.

XXIV

His neighbour uses the wrong colour-coded bin-bags and the police couldn't care less.

XXV

He'd like to be on television just once, even if it meant making a complete turd of himself.

XXVI

Like a peeled onion he attracts germs, thus sparing his colleagues from disease.

XXVII

They appreciate his custom, they thank him for continuing to hold.

XXVIII

He avoids leading the brainstorming session for fear of elementary spelling mistakes.

XXIX

Maybe it's the coffee he's drinking. He should change to a more recognised brand.

XXX

He saw Princess Anne going past in a car—does that count?

XXXI

His only ornaments, the traffic cones he stole from a fatal accident when he was eight.

XXXII

He found the very image of the Virgin Mary in a baked potato, but he had to eat.

XXXIII

His one contact in the world of high finance goes and dies from a monkey bite.

XXXIV

He stands guard over the letterbox all night after the last fireworks display in his street.

XXXV

The foul breath of the fridge when he opens the door. Ditto the washing machine.

XXXVI

He doesn't feel close to people until he can say with certainty what their problems are.

XXXVII

Lord, he has eaten the cold ash from the hearth. Will that
suffice?

XXXVIII

It's a case of Tyrannosaurus Rex versus The Corduroy Kid:
the evolving peaks of his mountainous spine now noticeable
through his favourite jacket, his fabric of choice.

XXXIX

After years of solitude anything is possible—even a moustache.

XL

Oh to be wassailed like the apple tree, his lowest branch
dipped in a cider pail, companionable villagers kissing his
roots, throwing hand-made tokens of good luck into his
arms, singing and singing his name.

The Patent

i.m. Michael Donaghy

Last night in the shed he was working late,
perfecting light,

inventing the light bulb that lasts and lasts.
He believes in lamps

which as well as giving an instant shine
will illuminate over and over again

and far from being dim, the prototypes
are surprisingly bright,

and functional too, being fused
for domestic use.

But the light-bulb people are up in arms.
They haven't come this far

to be put in the shade, outshone
by a light whose licence they claim to own,

by a lamp they invented themselves,
then shelved.

So they're hitting back with a cunning device
which works in reverse,

which soaks up colours
and light until darkness occurs.

Known as Obscurity Bulbs
these dense, inky blobs

are available in a range of marques
from *Evening Murk*

to *Endless Midnight of Fathomless Depth*.
They're very left

field, almost like art,
and the trade magazines are pushing them hard.

Which leads us straight
to a city, a town, a blotted-out street,

whose residents blink
at the clues in the crossword, squint at the book

they're trying to read.
Although . . . in a garden shed across the road

there's a glint. A man works late
perfecting light,

his hand cupped like some secretive priest
of the ancient past

protecting a flame in the night.
His face in the bulb of glass, like an astronaut.

The Stint

That term, what was the use?
Everyone knew better. Even the baseball hat
in the fibreglass parking booth could talk the talk
and was picking a hole in somebody's work
with his free hand. Where was the sense?

It was a season of cull.
Sharpshooters strolled across gardens and lawns,
inflicting daylight on the inner thoughts of doe and buck.
From the sitting position, squirrels were picked off
from the back porch, for fun or luck.

Power-walking was the done thing.
In headphones, jobbing pedestrians muscled past,
moved ahead without breaking sweat. Not that the world
was numb: static leapt from hand to hand, sparking
the odd response. But nevertheless.

In the landmass beyond, pesticides, herbicides,
God-knows-what had trickled through the crust of hogs and
spuds
and blunted the water supply. Uptown, local celebrities
rinsed their hair in vinegar wine
to leach out the suds.

In the suburbs, squad cars
ran down unpaid library fines and overdue books.
All night, freight trains moaned, ghosted the streets
hauling mile after mile
of actual goods.

And then the birds.
They circled the park—that picnic blanket
of freeze-dried grass between Washington, College,

Johnson and Dodge—a murder of rooks, streaming
from under the hem of the sky,

inverted air offering
effortless flight. Endless, unapplauding hands
in black gloves looking for somewhere to land,
and an English scarecrow directly below,
singled out, running for home.

Punishment

Kin though we are, should one of your good selves
cross the line, stray from those darkened, end-stopped
ginnels and ways, step from the switchbacks

into our lamp-lit lanes, our metalled streets
with their sleeping policemen and cats' eyes,
with their blue plaques and Neighbourhood Watch signs,

then an unwritten rule comes into play.
Kith though we are, we point to our titles
and deeds, and the right is reserved to bring

an axe-head down on a trespasser's wrist.
Here's how it works: before our hatchet-man
sizes the flesh—like a family butcher

pricing his cut—we ask for your best hand,
right or left. Tell us the truth and we hack
the other mitt. Lie and we dock both.

Remember these school desks? The top flips up
and doubles as a chopping board. Now drop
those fancy cufflinks in the inkwell, friend, and sign off.

Poetry

In Wells Cathedral there's this ancient clock,
three parts time machine, one part zodiac.
Every fifteen minutes, knights on horseback
circle and joust, and for six hundred years

the same poor sucker riding counterways
has copped it full in the face with a lance.
To one side, some weird looking guy in a frock
back-heels a bell. Thus the quarter is struck.

It's empty in here, mostly. There's no God
to speak of—some bishops have said as much—
and five quid buys a person a new watch.
But even at night with the great doors locked

chimes sing out, and the sap who was knocked dead
comes cornering home wearing a new head.

from Sir Gawain and the Green Knight

The green man prepared, got into position,
bent forward, revealing a flash of green flesh
as he heaped his hair to the crown of his head;
the nape of his neck was now naked and ready.
Gawain grips the axe and heaves it up high—
plants his left foot firmly on the floor in front—
then swings it swiftly into the bare skin.
The sharpness of the blow split the spinal cord
and parted the fat and the flesh so far
that the bright steel blade bit into the floor.
The huge green head tumbled onto the earth
and the king's men kicked it as it clattered past.
Blood guttered from his body, bright against his green gown,
yet the man didn't shudder or stagger or sink
but leaped alive on those tree-trunk legs
and rummaged around, reached out at their feet,
copped hold of his head and lifted it high,
then strode to his steed and snatched the bridle,
stepped into the stirrup, swung into the saddle,
gripping with one hand—by his hair—his own head.
Then he settled himself in his seat with the ease
of a man unmarked, never mind being minus
          his head!
And when he wheeled about
his bloody neck still bled.
His point was proved. The court
was deadened now with dread.

For that scalp and skull now swung from his fist.
To the front of the table he turned the face
and it lifted its eyelids, stared straight ahead
and spoke this speech, which you'll hear for yourselves:
"Sir Gawain, be wise enough to keep your word
and faithfully follow me until I'm found,

as you vowed in this hall within hearing of these horsemen.
You're charged with getting to the Green Chapel,
to reap what you've sown. You'll rightfully receive
the justice you deserve just as January dawns.
Men know my name as the Green Chapel Knight
and even a fool couldn't fail to find me.
So come, or be called a coward for ever."
With a tug of the reins he twisted around
and, head still in hand, galloped out of the hall,
so the flame in the flint shot fire from the hooves.
Which kingdom he came from they hadn't a clue,
no more than they knew where he headed for next.
        And then?
Well, with the green man gone
they grinned and laughed again,
and yet such goings on
were magic to those men.

After the Hurricane

Some storm that was, to shoulder-charge the wall
in my old man's back yard and knock it flat.
But the greenhouse is sound, that chapel of glass
we glazed one morning. We glazed *with* morning.
And so is the hut. And so is the shed.

We sit in the ruins and drink. He smokes.
Back when, we would have built that wall again.
But today it's enough to drink and smoke
amongst mortar and bricks, here at the empire's end.

The Spelling

I left a spelling at my father's house
written in small coins on his front step.
It said which star I was heading for next,
which channel to watch, which button to press.
I should have waited, given that spelling
a voice, but I was handsome and late.

While I was gone he replied with pebbles
and leaves at my gate. But a storm got up
from the west, sluicing all meaning and shape.

I keep his broken spelling in a tin,
tip it out on the cellar floor, hoping
a letter or even a word might form.
And I am all grief, staring through black space
to meet his eyes, trying to read his face.

Fisherwood

There's no reply. I am too late.
But every son carries a key

on a string, noosed around his neck.
I'll let myself in and I'll wait.

So did you just leave? Because here
on the arm of the chair there's heat—

the warm hob left by a hot drink . . .
No, just the sun, the fingerprint

of our nearest star, reaching this far.
I'll sit for a while and I'll weep;

under my eyelids, northern lights
and solar flares shimmer and rage.

The Stake-Out

They're watching the house from the woods.
They're staring through leaves, hanging back
in the dark alcoves between trees.
They think I can't see them. I can't.

They're watching the house from the woods.
I'm lying low behind the couch,
stooping under the windowsill.
I won't be seen dead in the porch.

I've turned out the lights. For supper
it's cold, black meat straight from the can.
I don't sleep, I nap, my big toe
wired by dental floss to the latch.

They're watching the house from the woods.
I crawl with a knife in my teeth
to the phone, slit its throat, throttle
a gas jet, gag the letterbox.

I've closed down, shut up shop. I shit
in the cavity wall, exhale
in a cupboard and lock the door.
I'd eat my tongue rather than speak.

Thermal cameras can squint through bricks
but I'm in the fridge, my heartbeat
sluggish, faint, breathing my own breath.
A dark star pulses in deep space.

They're watching the house from the woods.
I'm two eyes in a face of soot.
I haven't blinked for a whole hour.
The moment they see me I'll shoot.

RSPB Big Garden Birdwatch,
29–30 January 2005

Not the perched, anthracite, anvil form
of a jackdaw, rook or carrion crow
on a sycamore branch, but the limp, snagged,
wind-shredded flag of a carrier bag
on an overhead wire in wasteland beyond.

Encapsulate

I
Was anything ever more wholly dead
than the birdless, blown-out shell of an egg?

II
Like the thousands hauled from the caravan
of an Anglian man, whose arm had snaked

across the region's reserves and estates.
In his possession the day he was copped:

containers, maps and an egg-blowing kit
plus eggs of the corncrake and avocet.

In his client's defence, said his advocate,

III
the habit was handed down in the blood,
father to son. Here was a man at one

with the countryside, with the fens and heaths
(and I'm quoting here) which he *lived and breathed;*

whose brother had drowned at the age of twelve
while raiding the cribs of waders or gulls.

Inhale, and the yolk flows into the lungs.

IV
Like these green-brown, brown-green nightingale eggs

in their huddled clutches of four, five, six,
in their pigeon holes and cotton-wool nests.

V
Or presented here like a lover's gift—
this scuttled nightjar egg, its outer wall

speckled and flecked, its inner world stippled
with the dots and dabs of nature boy's spittle.

Pheasants

I *Hen*

One at dawn within yards of the back door,
strutting and starched, pretending not to look.
Then it was all legs and off with a flap,
like the vicar's wife from the village hall,
high-tailing away from the bric-a-brac stall
as her husband stood there baring his soul.

II *Cock*

One at dusk, skulking behind next door's hut.
Flushed by the clunk of the latch it rears up,
a tantrum of colours and royal plumes,
then stomps off—*fuck, fuck, fuck*—cursing its luck.
As if such feathers weren't bad enough, but
groomed in the style of a magistrate's hat . . .

III *Brace*

Slow on the uptake, slow to take a hint,
I'm still at a loss as to what was meant
by the pair that swept past the window frame
in the same split-second of bated breath
in which the presenter, announcing his death,
forgot then remembered the poet's name.

IV *Flock*

Grown just for the pot, they number no more
than those who somehow escaped being shot.
The hens like widows of war—dowdy, drawn,
the cocks rakish and loud, like local spivs
who avoided the call, or glaring and lost,
like those who served and came home afterwards.

Learning by Rote

Dear Sir, in class I was the backwards boy
who wrote cack-handedly. You made me sign
my name—but in reverse—ten thousand times.
Because the punishment must fit the crime.

Simon Armitage, Simon Armitage
at break time, after school, four thousand, five,
Simon Armitage, Simon Armitage
eight thousand, nine, until my father's note:

Enough's enough. Now leave the boy alone.

Forgotten. Buried in the past. Except
this loose-leaf jotter came to light today,
crammed with some Latin-looking motto, page
on page on page on page, the words

Simon Armitage, Simon Armitage

and then the sudden, childish urge to wave
this wad of mirror-writing in your face.
And then again, and then again, and then
again, again, again, again.

The Final Straw

Corn, like the tide coming in. Year on year,
fat, flowing grain, as it had always grown.
We harvested clockwise, spiralling home
over undulations of common land
till nothing remained but a hub of stalks
where the spirit of life was said to lurk.

So childless couples were offered the scythe—
the men invited to pocket the seed,
the women to plait dolls from the last sheaf.

But a Spix's macaw flapped from the blade,
that singular bird of the new world, one
of a kind. A rare sight. And a sign, being
tail feathers tapering out of view, being

blueness lost in the sun, being gone.